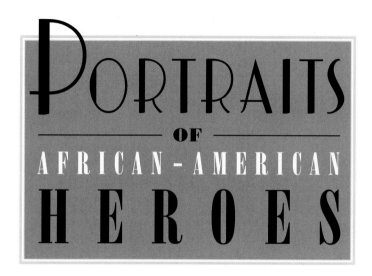

Portraits
OF
AFRICAN-AMERICAN
HEROES

Tonya Bolden

paintings by
Ansel Pitcairn

PUFFIN BOOKS

For Louise "MaLou" Bolden,
whom I count among my heroes,
and my blessings
—T.B.

To my mother, Yvonne, with love
—A.P.

PUFFIN BOOKS
Published by the Penguin Group
Penguin Young Readers Group, 345 Hudson Street, New York, New York 10014, U.S.A.
Penguin Group (Canada), 10 Alcorn Avenue, Toronto, Ontario, Canada M4V 3B2
(a division of Pearson Penguin Canada Inc.)
Penguin Books Ltd, 80 Strand, London WC2R 0RL, England
Penguin Ireland, 25 St Stephen's Green, Dublin 2, Ireland
(a division of Penguin Books Ltd)
Penguin Group (Australia), 250 Camberwell Road, Camberwell, Victoria 3124, Australia
(a division of Pearson Australia Group Pty Ltd)
Penguin Books India Pvt Ltd, 11 Community Centre, Panchsheel Park, New Delhi - 110 017, India
Penguin Group (NZ), Cnr Airborne and Rosedale Roads, Albany, Auckland 1310,
New Zealand (a division of Pearson New Zealand Ltd)
Penguin Books (South Africa) (Pty) Ltd, 24 Sturdee Avenue, Rosebank, Johannesburg 2196, South Africa

Registered Offices: Penguin Books Ltd, 80 Strand, London WC2R 0RL, England

First published in the United States of America by Dutton Children's Books,
a division of Penguin Young Readers Group, 2003
Published by Puffin Books, a division of Penguin Young Readers Group, 2005

9 10

Text copyright © Tonya Bolden, 2003
Illustrations copyright © Ansel Pitcairn, 2003
All rights reserved

THE LIBRARY OF CONGRESS HAS CATALOGED THE DUTTON EDITION AS FOLLOWS:
Bolden, Tonya.
Portraits of African-American heroes/text by Tonya Bolden; paintings by Ansel Pitcairn.—1st ed.
p. cm.
Contents: Frederick Douglass—Matthew Henson—W. E. B. Du Bois—Mary McLeod Bethune—
Bessie Coleman—Paul Robeson—Satchel Paige—Thurgood Marshall—Pauli Murray—
Joe Louis—Gwendolyn Brooks—Jacob Lawrence—Dizzy Gillespie—Shirley Chisholm—
Malcolm X—Martin Luther King, Jr.—Charlayne Hunter-Gault—Judith Jamison—
Ruth Simmons—Ben Carson.
ISBN: 0-525-47043-3 (hc)
1. African Americans—Biography—Juvenile literature. [1. African Americans—Biography.
2. Heroes.] I. Pitcairn, Ansel, ill. II. Title.
E185.96.B58 2003
920'.009296073—dc21 2002075911

Puffin Books ISBN 978-0-14-240473-7

Manufactured in China

CONTENTS

Introduction

Books are collaborations among many people. The first few who worked on this book were the editor, the artist, and the author. Each has something to say regarding the book.

The editor: I am interested in stories, and every book has one. The idea for doing a book of portraits of some African-American heroes began, as many books do, in an editor's office. Ansel Pitcairn came to show me his portfolio. In the trove of gorgeous work, I particularly admired his portrait of Joe Louis. Then I saw those of Thurgood Marshall, Malcolm X, and astronaut Mae Jemison. A book took form in my mind, and I asked if he wanted to do portraits of others. A collection of such portraits, matched with a strong text and a beautiful design, would make a striking and valuable book. We decided on twenty subjects.

The artist: But how do you choose twenty from such a vast field of African-Americans who have accomplished so much and inspired so many? Not easily.

Shirley Chisholm was the springboard for a series of portraits I had started some time back. About twenty-five years ago, she came to lecture my grade-school class on the importance of education and of pursuing personal goals. I wasn't aware of her political courage at the time, but her charisma left an invaluable impression that remains with me today.

For this book, author and friend Tonya Bolden and I, along with our editor, Lucia Monfried, did a lot of brainstorming on achievers in a variety of arenas, from arts and education to sports and politics. With so many people to choose from, the selection process was a sometimes stormy back-and-forth as we sought a way to reach an easy blend and balance of people we count among our heroes and inspirations. The final twenty we selected say something about those who did the choosing—our choices include personal favorites—at the same time that they offer profound lessons on living.

The author: I have always found it both comforting and strengthening to journey into the lives of people of positive ambitions who made the most of their potential.

Arctic explorer Matthew Henson and aviator Bessie Coleman inspire us to not shrink from adventure. Painter Jacob Lawrence, poet Gwendolyn Brooks, musician Dizzy Gillespie, and dancer Judith Jamison speak to us of the immense rewards, for self and society, that can come of giving free rein to our creative energies. Frederick Douglass, Paul Robeson, and Martin Luther King, Jr., challenge us to put convictions above convenience. Writer-scholar-activist W.E.B. Du Bois and writer-lawyer-educator-activist-minister Pauli Murray do the same, as they remind us that we need not limit ourselves to a single pursuit. Mary McLeod Bethune (school founder and so much more), lawyer Thurgood Marshall, and Ansel's great inspiration, politician Shirley Chisholm, are sterling examples of living not for oneself alone. They are also studies in true grit, as are the others in this book: surgeon Ben Carson, educator Ruth Simmons, journalist Charlayne Hunter-Gault, boxing great Joe Louis, baseball legend Satchel Paige, and Malcolm X.

The paintings tell a story, too. Mary McLeod Bethune wears pearls; Charlayne Hunter-Gault wears cornrows. Malcolm X, his hat tipped forward, stares out as if trying to read the future; Frederick Douglass seems to be burning with the injustices of the past and present. Paul Robeson projects a brooding intensity in one of his roles; Judith Jamison dances fervently against the backdrop of a giant moon.

My profiles in fortitude, sacrifice, and vision are far from in-depth. My aim was to capture something of the essence of these twenty people. Once upon a time they were boys and girls who could have opted to be mediocre, but did not. They could have listened to the lies others spread about their inherent value: they could have believed that because they were black or female or poor (or all three) they dared not strive to amount to something.

Now you, the reader, become part of the collaboration. It is our hope that these paintings and words prompt you to learn more about the lives and legacies of these twenty personalities. May this book move you to think long about what it means to be a hero and the varieties of heroism, and spark a new or renewed appreciation of your heroes whether they be parents, grandparents, neighbors, teachers, or people you know only from afar. May you also be motivated to live a true life, and leave a legacy that will inspire future generations to do likewise.

FREDERICK DOUGLASS

For twenty years, the man born Frederick Augustus Washington Bailey suffered days and nights of hunger, ragged clothing, beatings, and thousands of hours of work without pay. Yet he refused to believe himself inferior; he refused to allow his spirit to be conquered—he refused to be a slave.

Frederick was about nine years old when he made his first strike for freedom: learning, on the sly, to read. He devoured any book or newspaper he could get his hands on so as to improve his grasp of the world around him—and the words around him, too.

Abolitionist. This was one of the words that bewildered young Frederick. "If a slave ran away...or if a slave killed his master, set fire to a barn, or did any thing very wrong in the mind of a slaveholder, it was spoken of as the fruit of *abolition.*" When he set about learning the word's meaning, "the dictionary afforded me little or no help." *Abolition*, he read, was the "act of abolishing," but, alas, "I didn't know what was to be abolished."

Everything clicked when young Frederick read a newspaper article about petitions to abolish slavery in Washington, D.C., and slave trading within America. "From this time I understood the words *abolition* and *abolitionist*, and always drew near when that word was spoken, expecting to hear something of importance to myself and fellow-slaves." Understanding fueled hope, resolve, courage.

- **BORN:** *Mid-February 1818 (?), in Talbot County, Maryland*
- **DIED:** *February 20, 1895, in Washington, D.C.*

Douglass made his great escape when living in Baltimore, having been rented to a shipbuilder. September 3, 1838, was the day he slipped away with a free seaman's identification papers and all "rigged out in sailor style."

A train to Havre de Grace, Maryland. A ferry across the Susquehanna River. A train to Wilmington, Delaware. A steamboat to Philadelphia, Pennsylvania—at last he was on free soil—and then on, by train, to New York City, where he connected with Underground Railroad worker David Ruggles and other black abolitionists. With their help, he made his way farther north to New Bedford, Massachusetts, where he found work at a shipyard. To elude slave hunters, he settled on a new surname.

"The American people have this to learn: Where justice is denied, where poverty is enforced, where ignorance prevails, and where any one class is made to feel that society is in an organized conspiracy to oppress, rob, and degrade them, neither persons nor property will be safe." —*Frederick Douglass*

Keeping his own freedom wasn't Frederick Douglass's only concern: his heart ached for the millions of enslaved children and adults in America. So he did something about it—he became an *abolitionist*.

Douglass battled slavery as a public speaker. He was halting, nervous, awkward at first. The more he spoke, however, the more eloquent and compelling he became. By the mid-1840s, he was among the most renowned antislavery lecturers—motivating others to become abolitionists; fortifying those already protesting slavery; raising money for the printing of pamphlets, for purchasing people out of captivity, and for the activities of the Underground Railroad.

Douglass made a mark with the pen as well. His first autobiography, *Narrative of the Life of Frederick Douglass*, was a brisk seller when published in 1845. Douglass also wrote numerous articles for various newspapers, including the one he cofounded in 1847, the *North Star*—so named because it was this star, poised almost directly over the North Pole, that many people escaping slavery in the South relied on to stay on course in their journey north to freedom.

When the Civil War broke out in 1861, Douglass prayed that it would result in the end of slavery in America. Without a doubt, he rejoiced mightily when, on January 1, 1863, President Abraham Lincoln issued the Emancipation Proclamation, which freed the roughly three million people enslaved in Confederate territory. And when, in December 1865—eight months after the Civil War ended—slavery was abolished throughout America by the Thirteenth Amendment to the United States Constitution, Douglass's whole soul sighed, *Glory, Glory Hallelujah!*

Naturally, Douglass rejoiced some more when blacks were granted citizenship (Fourteenth Amendment, 1868) and when black men gained the right to vote (Fifteenth Amendment, 1870). Still, discrimination against blacks remained severe. So Douglass stayed the crusader: he refused to hold his tongue or rest his pen. And his own was never his only cause. He roared against the oppression of all people.

It was because of his years of support for the women's movement that the seventy-seven-year-old Frederick Douglass was an honored guest and featured speaker at a National Council of Women gathering in Washington, D.C., in February 1895.

Later that day, this majestic man had a heart attack and passed away, leaving a legacy that would inspire others, generation after generation, to devote their time and talents to making America a more noble nation.

■   ■   ■

MATTHEW HENSON

On April 6, 1909, Matthew Alexander Henson, the son of Maryland sharecroppers, was on top of the world, literally. This was the day that he and Robert Edwin Peary—a white man—along with four Inuit aides, became the first people to set foot on the North Pole. Many scholars contend that had it not been for Matt Henson, Peary, the expedition's commander, would never have fulfilled his dream of planting an American flag at the North Pole.

Henson had been indispensable to Peary for years. The two first met in 1887. At the time, Henson, a former seafarer who had traveled to Asia, Europe, and Africa, was working in a men's-clothing store in Washington, D.C. Peary, a lieutenant in the navy's Civil Engineer Corps, came in, shopping for a hat. He was also in need of a personal servant for a journey to Central America (to scout out a route for a canal in Nicaragua that would connect the Atlantic and Pacific Oceans).

During their encounter in the store, Peary sized up Henson as intelligent and industrious. For his part, Henson was more than eager to embark on another adventure.

During the seven-month Central American expedition, Henson proved himself so sturdy and capable—and so much more than a personal servant—that Peary asked him to join him on a journey to the Arctic.

Between 1891 and 1906, Peary led several expeditions to the Far

- **BORN**: *August 8, 1866, in Charles County, Maryland*
- **DIED**: *March 9, 1955, in New York City*

North. Triumphs included reaching the northern point of Greenland in 1892 (and proving that Greenland was an island) and coming within 175 miles of the North Pole in 1906. Henson was with Peary on all these expeditions, and he would accompany him on what Peary vowed would be his final attempt to reach the North Pole, the last four hundred miles of which would be a trek across the frozen Arctic Ocean.

As before, Henson was the only black member of Peary's expedition, which set sail from New York City in early July 1908. They docked west of the northern tip of Greenland, at Cape Sheridan on Ellesmere Island, in early September. Then came the westward march to the island's Cape Columbia, where the party readied themselves for the final push in late February 1909.

> "There can be no vision to the man the horizon of whose vision is limited by the bounds of self.... The great accomplishments of the world have been achieved by [those] who had high ideals and... great visions. The path is not easy, the climbing is rugged and hard, but the glory at the end is worthwhile."
> —*Matthew Henson*

Henson's work included building igloos; building and repairing sledges that could bear upwards of five hundred pounds of provisions; hunting for musk ox and reindeer; training the husky wolf dogs; breaking trails with a pickax; and navigating sledges over ten-, twenty-, sixty-foot-high ice ridges.

Henson stayed strong through blizzards and blistering, piercing winds; through freezing temperatures that dipped, at times, to nearly sixty below zero; through a near fatal fall through a patch of thin ice. Through it all, Henson never flagged in his admiration for and loyalty to Peary, who often had to ride in a sledge because he had lost several toes to frostbite during a previous expedition.

At the outset, it was clear that not everyone would accompany Peary to the very end of the journey. Trails would be broken, and supplies would be stashed in igloos along the way. At various points, one by one or two by two, team members would return to the ship. When Peary set off for the last leg

of the journey on April 1, 1909, he chose Matt Henson as his mainstay.

A few days later, Henson wrote in his autobiography, "the commander gave the word, 'We will plant the stars and stripes—*at the North Pole!'* and it was done; on the peak of a huge . . . floeberg the glorious banner was unfurled to the breeze, and as it snapped and crackled with the wind, I felt a savage joy and exultation. Another world's accomplishment was done and finished."

After their return to America, Peary minimized Henson's contributions to the expedition. Peary resented—and even tried to stop—Henson's speaking engagements on the subject. Outside the black community, Henson went forgotten and unrewarded.

Henson did eventually get his due. In 1944, the United States Navy presented him with a medal acknowledging him as codiscoverer of the North Pole. On April 6, 1988, Henson and his wife, both buried in a cemetery in New York City, were reburied near Peary and his wife in Arlington National Cemetery, where since 1864, a host of American heroes (Joe Louis and Thurgood Marshall among them) have been laid to rest.

■ ■ ■

W.E.B. DU BOIS

William Edward Burghardt Du Bois—that is the full name of the man known in his youth as "Willie" and later in life as "W.E.B."

His drive and talents were very apparent when he was growing up in a tiny black community—roughly fifty people—in a cozy Massachusetts town with a population of about five thousand (mostly Irish, Dutch, and German). By the age of thirteen, Willie was giving speeches and participating in debates at town meetings. By age fifteen, he was a correspondent for the *New York Globe,* a daily newspaper edited by the once enslaved activist T. Thomas Fortune.

In school, Willie was stellar—from elementary school through his days at Great Barrington High, where at his graduation ceremonies in 1884 he gave a stirring speech on the white social reformer Wendell Phillips. Willie wanted to be like Wendell Phillips and like his other heroes, who included Frederick Douglass and T. Thomas Fortune: he wanted to "uplift" his race. In preparation for this, he set his sights on doing what very few people did in those days—go to college.

Through scholarships (and part-time and summer jobs), Willie obtained an excellent education, beginning at Fisk University in Nashville, Tennessee, where he was editor of the school's newspaper, the *Fisk Herald.* He capped his education as the first black person to earn a Ph.D. from Harvard University, in Cambridge, Massachusetts.

Sociology, history, chemistry, geology, philosophy, economics, politics,

- **BORN**: *February 23, 1868, in Great Barrington, Massachusetts*
- **DIED**: *August 27, 1963, in Accra, Ghana*

literature, Latin, Greek, and more—by the late 1890s, W. E. B. Du Bois had a head full of knowledge, along with an exquisite command of the English language, both written and oral. All this he put to excellent use: challenging his country to be righteous and mustering other blacks to, in the words of Frederick Douglass, "Agitate! Agitate! Agitate!" for just and fair treatment.

Du Bois agitated in various ways. He enlightened younger minds as a professor at Atlanta University and at other colleges. He played a critical role in several organizations, including the National Association for the Advancement of Colored People (NAACP), which he cofounded in 1909. More than thirty years later, he became an integral part of the Council on African Affairs, cofounded by his friend Paul Robeson.

Du Bois's newspaper experience as a teen and young adult gave him the confidence and know-how to launch several periodicals, including the NAACP's magazine, *Crisis*. Over the years, Du Bois contributed countless essays and articles to other magazines and newspapers.

> "I believe in pride of race and lineage and self: in pride of self so deep as to scorn injustice to other selves."
> —*W.E.B. Du Bois*

Du Bois's writing was not limited to short works. Along with several plays and novels, he produced dozens of books of nonfiction. Among the most important are the seven-hundred-plus-page *Black Reconstruction in America: An Essay Toward a History of the Part Which Black Folk Played in the Attempt to Reconstruct Democracy in America, 1860–1880*, and his best-known book, *The Souls of Black Folk*, a collection of poignant essays on the black experience.

There's no counting how many marches and rallies Du Bois participated in, how many speeches and lectures he gave all over the world against lynching, against discrimination and segregation of blacks, against the European exploitation of Africa, against corporations exploiting workers.

Du Bois paid a price for his activism. With each passing year, he was

seen as more and more "radical"—too radical—and "dangerous" by the U.S. government. Because of his involvement in the international peace movement and his support for the Soviet Union, Du Bois was arrested in 1951, when he was in his eighties, and then indicted for being an unregistered propaganda agent for the Soviet Union. The case was dismissed, but government harassment continued. His mail was read. FBI agents tried to dig up dirt on him. For a time, his passport was revoked, limiting his ability to travel abroad. Many people became afraid to associate with him, lest they, too, be labeled "radical."

By 1961, Du Bois had had enough of America. At the invitation of Kwame Nkrumah, the president of Ghana, he moved to this first sub-Saharan African nation to gain its independence (from Britain in 1957). In Ghana, Du Bois began work on his most ambitious project, the *Encyclopaedia Africana,* a multivolume compendium of information about Africa and the African diaspora.

W. E. B. Du Bois died before completing his encyclopedia, on the eve of the historic March on Washington for Jobs and Freedom, where Martin Luther King, Jr., delivered his famous "I Have a Dream" speech.

■ ■ ■

MARY MCLEOD BETHUNE

My feet are sore now, my limbs are tired, my mind weary. I have gone over hills and valleys, everywhere, begging for nickels and dimes that have paid for this soil, for these buildings, for this equipment that you find here."

Mary McLeod Bethune uttered these words in 1923 at the creation of Bethune-Cookman College in Daytona Beach, Florida. This college was a merger of Darnell Cookman Institute, a school for boys in Jacksonville, Florida, and Bethune's Daytona Normal and Industrial Training School, originally for girls.

Bethune had started her school in 1904, in a shack, with a handful of students. Instead of focusing on how threadbare her school was, Bethune envisioned how strong it could become. And she knew that this would require hard work, to which she was no stranger.

As a child—one of more than a dozen children born to parents once enslaved—she picked cotton, plowed ground, and did other heavy work on her family's farm; she helped her mother lug laundry back and forth to customers; she walked long miles to school.

As a young woman, she did domestic work to first make it through Scotia Seminary (today Barber-Scotia College) in Concord, North Carolina, from which she graduated in 1893, and then through two years at Moody Bible Institute in Chicago, Illinois.

- **BORN:** *July 10, 1875, near Mayesville, South Carolina*
- **DIED:** *May 18, 1955, in Daytona Beach, Florida*

Her great hope was to become a missionary in Africa. When the Presbyterian Board of Missions refused to send black missionaries to Africa, and she could find no other church to sponsor her, she became a teacher. She taught at several schools in the South before starting her own school in Daytona Beach.

"We burned logs and used the charred splinters as pencils. For ink we mashed up elderberries," said Bethune, recalling her school's early days. She was a genius at making the most of whatever materials were at hand. She was a marvel of not giving in to discouragement. And she was not too proud to go "begging" for nickels and dimes to keep her school alive.

"If I have a legacy to leave my people, it is my philosophy of living and serving.... I pray now that my philosophy may be helpful to those who share my vision of a world of peace, progress, brotherhood, and love." —Mary McLeod Bethune

In time, people not only in Daytona Beach, but elsewhere in Florida and around the nation, recognized Bethune's dedication and the fine job she was doing when it came to educating the young.

People were glad to donate nickels, dimes, dollars, and, eventually, thousands to her school. By the time Bethune's school merged with the Cookman Institute, it had several hundred students, a farm (on which students grew food for themselves and to sell), and several stately buildings. By then, the forty-eight-year-old Bethune may have been footsore and weary, but she was not ready to rest. She stayed at the helm of Bethune-Cookman for another twenty-odd years. What's more, she kept busy on other fronts.

The list is long. It includes serving as president, from 1924 to 1928, of the organization whose motto is "Lifting As We Climb": the National Association of Colored Women. Its mission: "to participate in and support all causes working in the interest of the advancement of the Negro population as a whole and of women in particular."

One of Bethune's greatest achievements was founding, in 1935, the

National Council of Negro Women (NCNW), over which she presided until 1949. Through the NCNW, scores of women's organizations could pool their resources and thus work more effectively on funding schools and recreational facilities and on supporting other campaigns to improve the quality of life for multitudes of children and adults.

Bethune also worked on behalf of black social and economic advancement within the federal government. She was an organizer and leading member, from 1936 to 1943, of President Franklin Roosevelt's Federal Council on Negro Affairs, known as the "Black Cabinet." Roosevelt also appointed her director of the National Youth Administration's Division of Negro Affairs. Through this agency, thousands of young men and women received job training, jobs, and money for college.

By the mid-twentieth century, Bethune was among the most prominent and admired women in America. During her lifetime, and down through the years, people of insight and vision have told the children in their lives that Mary McLeod Bethune is the kind of person they should strive to be when they grow up.

■　■　■

BESSIE COLEMAN

TELL THEM ALL THAT AS SOON AS I CAN WALK I'M GOING TO FLY!" This was the start of a telegram stunt pilot Bessie Coleman sent to a newspaper in late February 1923, as she lay in a hospital in Santa Monica, California.

On the morning of February 4, while en route from Santa Monica to Los Angeles, Coleman's biplane, a "Jenny" (as Curtiss JN-4s were known), let her down. Shortly after takeoff, the motor stalled and the plane nose-dived—plummeting three hundred feet to the ground. Along with cuts and bruises on her face, Coleman had damaged ribs and a broken leg.

Those who believed Coleman would never fly again seriously underrated her gumption. Bessie Coleman, a fierce overcomer, wasn't about to let the California crack-up scare her out of the sky.

Coleman had grown up dirt poor in the tiny town of Waxahachie, Texas. At a young age, she was helping with the care of three younger siblings, picking cotton beneath a brutal sun, and making do with skimpy schooling at a one-room schoolhouse that was a four-mile walk from home. Still, this little girl vowed not to be kept down in life.

After trying to get a college education and failing because of lack of funds, in 1915 Coleman moved to Chicago, where two older brothers lived. In Chicago, Coleman picked up the art of manicure and worked at several barbershops frequented by influential black men. One of her customers

- **BORN:** *January 26, 1892, in Atlanta, Texas*
- **DIED:** *April 30, 1926, in Jacksonville, Florida*

was millionaire Robert Sengstacke Abbott, founder of the legendary *Chicago Defender*. It was through the pages of this newspaper that Coleman kept up with Eugene Bullard, a black American who had earned his wings in France and was serving in France's air corps. Coleman was fascinated with flight.

Two white men, Wilbur and Orville Wright, had made history with the first successful airplane flight in 1903. In 1911, a white woman, Harriet Quimby, had made history as America's first licensed female pilot. Bessie Coleman wanted to make aviation history, too.

When she could find no aviation school in America that would admit blacks, Coleman began taking French lessons and squirreling away all the money she could. In the fall of 1920, with moral and financial support from Robert Sengstacke Abbott and others, Coleman made her way to France. There she embarked on a seven-month course at one of the world's finest aviation schools and then passed the test that enabled her to return to America—with much fanfare—as the first black female aviator.

"If I can create the minimum of my plans and desires there shall be no regrets." —Bessie Coleman

By the time her plane crashed in California, Coleman had drawn huge crowds at air shows in Chicago, Boston, New York, and elsewhere in America. "Queen Bess, Daredevil Aviatrix," she was hailed.

She loved the applause. She loved being a celebrity. She loved sharpening her skills and showing them off. Even more, she loved the idea of starting an aviation school for blacks.

In the spring of 1925 Coleman set out on a tour of the South to raise money for her school, through lectures and air shows. She appeared in several cities in Texas—among them Waxahachie—and Georgia. After wintering in Chicago, she resumed her tour.

Coleman reached Jacksonville, Florida, in late April 1926, scheduled to perform as part of the May Day festivities. Folks couldn't wait to see her figure eights, barrel rolls, loop-the-loops, and a 2,500-foot parachute jump.

The day before the show, Coleman had another pilot wing her up so she could get a fix on a perfect point for her jump. She was not wearing her seat belt so that she could lean out for the best view.

Up, up, up went her Jenny. Up, up, up to 1,000 feet. Up, up, up to 2,000 feet, to 3,500 feet. Up, up—

The plane went out of control—nosedive, spiral, tailspin—and flipped upside down, flinging Coleman out into the sky. The pilot never righted the plane, crashing about 1,000 feet from where the lifeless body of Queen Bess lay.

Bessie Coleman left behind no memoirs, no large sums of money, no aviation school, nothing but her zest, her zeal—gold. She inspired many to reach higher, especially black women with an interest in flight, from Willa B. Brown, the first black woman to receive a commercial pilot's license (1937) and cofounder of an aviation school in Chicago, to Mae C. Jemison, the first black woman to voyage into outer space (1992).

■   ■   ■

PAUL ROBESON

Paul Leroy Bustill Robeson, the youngest of his parents' five children, was born two years after the United States Supreme Court dealt black America a devastating blow. The Court did this with its decision in the case *Plessy* v. *Ferguson*, ruling that having "separate but equal" facilities for whites and blacks (and other people of color) was constitutional. Facilities for blacks were never equal to those for whites, but segregation (from schools and parks to seating in movie theaters) became widespread, intensifying other forms of racism. This was the world in which Robeson grew up. And yet he thrived.

After graduating from high school with honors in 1915, and with a scholarship in hand, Robeson entered Rutgers College (now Rutgers University) in New Brunswick, New Jersey. Robeson was the third black person ever admitted to Rutgers, where he faced racism at every turn— from not being allowed to live in the student dormitory to being initially rejected by the fellows on the football team. Robeson rose above the hostility and became a fantastic achiever: more than a dozen varsity letters (in basketball, baseball, track, and football); a two-time All-American in football; a prizewinning orator; induction, in his junior year, into the top academic honor society, Phi Beta Kappa. He was valedictorian when he graduated, with honors.

Next, Robeson earned a law degree from New York City's Columbia

- **BORN:** *April 9, 1898, in Princeton, New Jersey*
- **DIED:** *January 23, 1976, in Philadelphia, Pennsylvania*

University Law School. A career in law couldn't, however, hold him. He was far more passionate about an acting and singing career, having dabbled in theater while in law school.

With his rich bass voice, a radiant, infectious smile, piercing eyes, and fine physique, Robeson mesmerized audiences not only on the stage but also on the screen, starring in about a dozen films. Most of the films were not magnificent: they presented black people as brutes or buffoons. Robeson, who would learn some twenty languages, frequently found himself uttering dialogue befitting an illiterate. He longed for film roles respectful of the intellects, imaginations, and souls of black folks.

All this Robeson conveyed as a concert singer. His specialty was the black sacred songs created in the days of slavery: the spirituals. By the early 1930s, Robeson had performed all across America and in England, France, the Soviet Union, and elsewhere in the world, soaring as one of the most famous performing artists of his day. But fame was not enough for Robeson.

"No one can leave a permanent mark on the world till he learns to be true to himself." —Paul Robeson

There came a day when Robeson refused to accept roles that were demeaning to black people, and when he refused to hold a concert if the audience was to be segregated: whites up front, blacks in the back or up in the balcony. Robeson also refused to stay silent about other wrongs, and he used his celebrity status to draw support to causes he believed just.

In interviews and at rallies, during his concerts and speaking engagements, Robeson spoke up for unions trying to get workers decent wages and safer working conditions; for African and Caribbean struggles against European rule; for an end to segregation and other racial injustices in America. He also spoke up for the Soviet Union at a time when America and that Communist country were archenemies. There came a day when government officials decided it was time for Paul Robeson to be silenced.

The FBI spied on Robeson; the State Department revoked his passport. By the mid-1950s Robeson was virtually an invisible man—no more bookings for concerts on major stages, no record deals, no appearances on top radio or television shows.

Robeson could have saved his fame and made a lot of money if only he had remained merely an entertainer. But Robeson could not turn on himself. Taking a stand was in his blood.

Robeson's father had taken a stand, at age fifteen, against his enslavement in North Carolina, by escaping it via the Underground  Railroad. Paul's forebears on his mother's side included Cyrus Bustill, cofounder of the first black self-help organization in America, the Free African Society (1787), and Grace Bustill Douglass, cofounder of the Philadelphia Female Anti-Slavery Society (1833).

For being true to his heritage, Paul Robeson lost a brilliant career, and the persecution took a toll on his health. A nervous breakdown, bouts of depression, and strokes were among his afflictions.

In 1998, the centennial of his birth, people across America sang Paul Robeson's praises. There were lectures on his artistry and his politics; showings of his films; a flood of newspaper and magazine articles; and assorted other tributes to his genius and his courage. By then, millions of people truly understood how badly he had been wronged and the huge price he had paid for standing his ground.

■   ■   ■

SATCHEL PAIGE

Many proclaim this Hall of Famer baseball's greatest pitcher, given how long he played professionally (until age fifty-nine) and how exciting he was to watch. And then there's his record. During his forty-plus years in baseball, Satchel Paige pitched roughly 2,500 games—more than anyone else in history—winning about 2,000. He could also boast of 55 no-hitters and more than 300 shutouts.

A bit over six foot three, with all-star feet (size fourteen), the lanky, wide-smiling Paige made history in July 1948. That's when the Cleveland Indians signed the forty-two-year-old right-hander. Paige became the twentieth century's first black pitcher on a major league team (a little over a year after Jackie Robinson made history as the twentieth century's first black in the majors). By 1948, Paige was already a newsmaker: before he played with the white "boys of summer," he was a star in the Negro Leagues.

When blacks were shut out of major league baseball in the late nineteenth century, the number of all-black teams increased. By the 1920s, there were enough teams for blacks to form leagues of their own. Thanks to the Negro Leagues, incredibly talented athletes had dynamite days on the diamond—home-run king Josh Gibson, the superfast center fielder James "Cool Papa" Bell, and Satchel Paige among the many.

From 1926 to 1948, Paige, notorious for jumping from team to team,

- **BORN:** *July 7, 1906, in Mobile, Alabama*
- **DIED:** *June 8, 1982, in Kansas City, Missouri*

played with a number of teams, including the Baltimore Black Sox, the Birmingham Black Barons, the Chattanooga Black Lookouts, the Kansas City Monarchs, and the Pittsburgh Crawfords. When folks heard a game was to feature Paige on the mound, there was sure to be a sell-out crowd.

Paige was a sensational sight to behold, psyching out—and striking out—many a fine batter with his clever kit of pitches: the "two hump blooper," the "drooper," the "jump ball," the "wobbly ball," his famed hesitation pitch, and the "bee ball," which whizzed by a batter in a blink. Paige's extravagant "windmill" windup was a hoot for all. As were the tall tales: did he really once hurl twenty straight pitches across a home plate consisting of a chewing gum wrapper?

> **"I was just as good as the white boys. I ain't going in the back door of the Hall of Fame."** —*Satchel Paige, in 1971, when the Baseball Hall of Fame initially proposed inducting him and other Negro Leagues greats into the Hall—but in a separate wing*

This legendary American didn't just play in America. In winter, like other baseball players, Paige was often where the weather was warm: in Cuba, the Dominican Republic, or Mexico, for instance. Playing abroad meant freedom from discrimination. When Negro Leaguers were on the road in America, unless they hit a town with a black-owned hotel and black-owned restaurants, they often ended up sleeping in their buses or cars, and taking meals by the side of a road.

Paige was in his late teens when he started on the road to pro ball in the early 1920s with the Mobile Tigers, a semipro team. He had taken a liking to baseball in elementary school and begun perfecting his pitching skills on a team from a reform school in Mount Meigs, Alabama. Paige had been sent to that school at age twelve for stealing toy rings from a store in his hometown, Mobile, Alabama.

Poverty was no excuse, but it was, in part, the reason young Paige swiped the trinkets. He was one of eleven children; and his father, a gardener, and his mother, a laundress, did not make enough money to

buy their children many treats.
Poverty was also the reason that
at age seven Paige was catching
nickels and dimes at the train
station by toting travelers'
luggage, often called satchels.
He was ingenious enough to rig
up, from a pole and some rope,
a contraption to carry lots of
luggage.

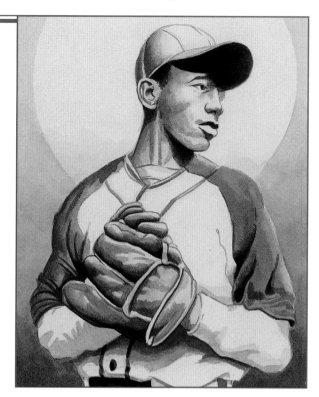

"You look like a walking
satchel tree!" a buddy exclaimed
one day. Pretty soon folks were
calling him Satchel and not his given name, Leroy. And when young Leroy
Robert Paige wasn't in school, at home doing chores, or "satcheling" at
the train station, he was often somewhere throwing rocks. Few things gave
the boy more pleasure than zapping cans and whatnot from tree limbs,
stumps, fence posts, and such. But he never imagined that his excellent
aim would bring him fame.

■ ■ ■

THURGOOD MARSHALL

When he was very young, his family called him "Goody," but that didn't last for long. Naughty, rambunctious, argumentative—these are just a few of the adjectives that fit the boy whose parents named him Thoroughgood, after a seafaring uncle. But the boy changed his name to Thurgood while in second grade—"I got tired of spelling all that, and shortened it." He stayed the rebel throughout his school days.

In high school, one punishment meted out to mischievous Marshall was lockdown in the basement with a copy of the United States Constitution: not until he had memorized a designated passage from the document could he return to class. Marshall must have been in trouble often, because he later claimed, "Before I left that school, I knew the whole thing by heart." Before he left that school, he also had proved himself a skilled debater, earned high grades, and thought about becoming a lawyer.

In the fall of 1925, Thurgood Marshall enrolled in Lincoln University in Oxford, Pennsylvania. Known as the "Black Princeton," this university's distinguished alumni included Paul Robeson's father. Among Marshall's classmates was Kwame Nkrumah, future president of Ghana.

At Lincoln, Marshall was a rowdy, cutting up at times with the much older student and already celebrated poet, Langston Hughes. But Marshall didn't make a waste of college. At Lincoln, he *learned*, refining his debating skills in the process.

- **BORN:** *July 2, 1908, in Baltimore, Maryland*
- **DIED:** *January 24, 1993, in Bethesda, Maryland*

After Lincoln, Marshall would have liked to attend the University of Maryland Law School, but he couldn't because the university did not admit black people. Instead, Marshall went to Howard University Law School in Washington, D.C., where he became the protégé of the law school's dean, Charles Hamilton Houston. This man had very high standards and was determined to train legal eagles who would use their skills in the service of social justice. Thanks to Houston's training, Thurgood Marshall became much more than a lawyer.

"Mr. Civil Rights" was what Marshall was called because of his relentless efforts to vanquish segregation through legal means—to make the Constitution stand up for blacks. Marshall embarked on this crusade in earnest in 1934, when he went to work for the National Association for the Advancement of Colored People (NAACP). At the time, Marshall's mentor, Charles Hamilton Houston, was chief counsel for the NAACP. Marshall became his top assistant, preparing and arguing cases where people's civil rights had been violated. One of Marshall's sweetest victories was the case *Murray* v. *Maryland* (1936), which resulted in the ruling that the University of Maryland had to stop excluding students solely on the basis of race.

"That he did what he could with what he had." —*Thurgood Marshall, when asked, in 1991, how he wished to be remembered*

When Houston retired in the late 1930s, Thurgood Marshall took his place, and shortly after he became the NAACP's chief counsel, Marshall transformed the legal division into a separate entity, the NAACP Legal Defense and Educational Fund (LDF).

The LDF filed lawsuits against race-based discrimination in an array of matters, including jury selection, housing, and public education. Marshall's ultimate school desegregation case was *Brown* v. *Board of Education*, a collection of cases from several states and Washington, D.C., which made its way to the highest court in the nation, the United States Supreme Court. The Court's decision, handed down on May 17, 1954, declared that segregation in public schools was unconstitutional, thus overturning the Supreme Court's ruling of 1896 in *Plessy* v. *Ferguson*.

The *Brown* decision laid a firm foundation for future legal assaults on segregation in recreational facilities, housing, sports arenas, and other places—and the eventual end of government-sanctioned segregation in America.

Marshall stayed in the forefront of the civil rights campaign for many more years, thoroughly convinced that legal challenges to discrimination were the soundest way to black empowerment. Although the LDF handled cases for Martin Luther King, Jr. (beginning with the 1955 Montgomery Bus Boycott), Marshall did not always agree with King's tactics. Marshall also vehemently opposed the call for black separatism by groups such as the Nation of Islam. He had an acute dislike for Malcolm X, and the feeling was mutual for a time. So Mr. Civil Rights was also Mr. Controversial, battling on several fronts—against white supremacists, fellow integrationists, and black separatists.

Marshall left the LDF in 1962, when President John F. Kennedy appointed him a federal judge. Three years later, President Lyndon Johnson appointed Marshall to the third highest legal post in the government: United States Solicitor General (the federal government's chief counsel, in essence). Marshall was the first black person to hold this position.

On October 2, 1967, the day he was sworn in as associate justice of the United States Supreme Court, Thurgood Marshall became another "first." No doubt about it, "Goody" did well in life; more important, he did good.

■   ■   ■

PAULI MURRAY

The woman born Anna Pauline Murray was never idle, ever striving, always on the move, accomplishing more than most people dare dream of tackling.

Writer. At age fifteen, she produced a novel, *Angel of the Desert*, which was serialized in the *Carolina Times*. Along with essays and articles for various periodicals, her later writings include a book Thurgood Marshall dubbed the "bible" for civil rights lawyers, *States' Laws on Race and Color* (1951); a history of her mother's family, *Proud Shoes* (1956); a collection of poetry, *Dark Testament* (1970); and her autobiography, *Song in a Weary Throat*, published two years after her death.

Lawyer. After earning a bachelor's degree at New York City's Hunter College (one of four blacks in a class of nearly 250), Murray applied to the University of North Carolina's law school, but she was rejected because, as the dean's letter stated, "members of your race are not admitted to the University." So instead, Murray attended Howard University's law school; she was the only female in the class of 1944 and graduated at the top of her class. After her application to Harvard University's law school was rejected (because the school refused to admit women), she earned a master's degree in law from the University of California at Berkeley in 1945. Some twenty years later, Murray earned a doctorate from Yale Law School, the first black person to do so.

- **BORN:** *November 20, 1910, in Baltimore, Maryland*
- **DIED:** *July 1, 1985, in Pittsburgh, Pennsylvania*

Activist. In the 1940s, working with the Workers Defense League, she raised funds for the legal aid of a black sharecropper in Virginia. This man, who Murray believed had had an unfair trial, had been sentenced to death for killing a white man.

Murray resisted "Jim Crow" (discriminatory laws and practices against blacks) by refusing to obey a Virginia bus driver's command to relinquish her seat to a white person and sit on a broken seat in the back of the bus. For her defiance, she spent three days in jail in the spring of 1940. While a student at Howard, she participated in sit-ins to integrate lunch counters in Washington, D.C., restaurants. It was her anger at antiblack laws and customs that had motivated her to go to law school in the first place.

In the 1960s and beyond, Murray spoke out about discrimination against women. "Jane Crow," she called it. One of her contributions to the women's movement was as a founding member of the National Organization for Women, in 1966, the most powerful women's rights organization of the late twentieth century.

> **"I speak for my race and my people— the human race and just people."**
> **—Pauli Murray**

Educator. In the 1930s, Murray taught in a New York City public school remedial-reading program. For about a year and a half in the early 1960s, she taught law at the Ghana School of Law in Accra. Her longest time of teaching was at Brandeis University in Waltham, Massachusetts, where she taught law and politics from 1968 to 1973.

Minister. In 1973, at age sixty-three, Murray became the oldest and the only black student at New York City's General Theological Seminary. There she earned a master of divinity degree and graduated, with honors, in 1976. The following year, Murray made history when she became the first black woman ordained priest in the Episcopal Church. Until she retired in the mid-1980s, Murray's ministry included aid and comfort to people in hospitals and to shut-ins.

Murray's achievements are all the more impressive given the traumas she suffered at a young age. Shortly before her fourth birthday, Pauli had to say good-bye to her home and immediate family in Baltimore, Maryland. She was being taken to Durham, North Carolina, to live with an aunt and her grandparents, while her five siblings were sent to live with other family members. The Murray children were to be raised by relatives because their mother, a nurse, had suffered a stroke and

died. Mr. Murray, a school principal, was unable to take care of his children because he was ailing from the aftereffects of typhoid fever. His health only worsened: when Pauli was six years old, he was committed to a hospital, where he was beaten to death by a racist hospital guard seven years later.

Young Pauli's Aunt Pauline, a teacher, lavished her with love and support, as did other relatives. They strengthened her with stories of the good and brave lives of many of her ancestors, including a grandfather who had fought in the Civil War and afterward taught recently freed people. Especially sustaining for Pauli were accounts of her parents' determination to live purposeful, productive lives. "Their striving to achieve," Murray wrote years later, "filled me with pride and incentive."

■ ■ ■

JOE LOUIS

W hen a reporter asked Joe Louis if, as a child, he had dreamed of being a champion—and a millionaire—this boxing great replied, "I couldn't dream that big."

He was born Joseph Louis Barrow to parents who struggled to support their eight children by sharecropping cotton. When Joe was two, his father (possibly an epileptic) was committed to a hospital for the mentally ill. When his mother remarried a man with several children, the new, larger family didn't fare much better. Young Joe's dreams were about such things as having more than one pair of shoes, a few changes of clothing, and a full belly.

In search of a better life, the family packed up for Detroit, Michigan, in 1926. There Joe's stepfather found a factory job, but then became one of the millions who lost their steady jobs during the Great Depression (1929–1939). During these lean years, Joe picked up odd jobs—one day moving crates at a produce market, another day (in those pre-refrigerator times) delivering fifty- to one-hundred-pound blocks of ice, often up four or five flights of stairs.

Joe was physically strong, but his academic abilities were not. A slight stutter made class participation a challenge. But he wasn't without talents: he was excellent at carpentry. He also tried his hand at the violin, at the urging of his mother, who managed to scrape together the fifty cents a week

- **BORN:** *May 13, 1914, in Lafayette, Alabama*
- **DIED:** *April 12, 1981, in Las Vegas, Nevada*

for his lessons. But then Joe started using his music-lesson money to rent a locker at a gym after a friend hooked him on boxing.

Joe wasn't a natural, but he had heart. He was willing to take instruction and criticism, and to *train*. In late 1932, he entered his first amateur fight and exited badly bruised, with the loser's take: a seven-dollar merchandise check (similar to a gift certificate).

In the spring of 1933—first round, second punch—his opponent was down for the count. Joe reveled in his twenty-five-dollar merchandise check and went on to rack up an amateur record of fifty wins out of fifty-four bouts, with forty-one knockouts. He also opted for the one-two-punch name of "Joe Louis."

> **"Don't jab at the target, jab through it."**
> **—Joe Louis**

After Joe Louis went pro in 1934, he astounded fight fans with his lightning left jab and wrecking-ball right, which he used against a string of formidable prizefighters. By February 1936 he had won twenty-seven bouts in a row, twenty-three of them KOs. Merchandise checks? Louis's winnings were $50,000, $60,000, and, in one fight, close to $250,000. Along the way, his tag became "The Brown Bomber."

Invincible? That's what he started to think. He slacked on his training, even as June 19, 1936, neared: the date of a bout at Yankee Stadium in the Bronx, New York. His opponent, Max Schmeling, was the pride of Nazi Germany, which was waging war in Europe and proclaiming the superiority of the Aryan race. When Schmeling KO'd Louis in the twelfth round, legions of white supremacists abroad and in America celebrated. Joe Louis was devasted, but he wasn't done.

Jabbing away at the speed bag, blitzing away at the punching bag, skipping rope, shadowboxing, running mile after mile—Louis trained, trained, trained, working up to a shot at the heavyweight champion, Jim Braddock.

Not since Jack Johnson, the twentieth century's first black heavyweight champ (1908–1915), had a black man been in a heavyweight title bout. It wasn't for a lack of contenders. Johnson, with his braggart's ways and his tendency to date white women, had enraged many white people. After Johnson, the bosses of boxing fixed it so that blacks were blocked from the top title bout. The Louis-Braddock match at Chicago's Comiskey Park, on June 22, 1937, was a breakthrough. A crowd of forty-five thousand packed the stadium, while tens of thousands caught the fight on the radio.

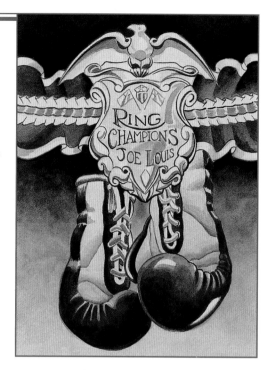

One minute, ten seconds into the eighth round, Louis landed a ripping right to Braddock's head and . . .

For black America, Joe Louis became so much more than a boxer. Joe Louis became its glory—its most visible symbol of black resilience and fortitude. With a black man as the Champ and such a celebrity, maybe white America would treat them with more respect, many blacks hoped.

They couldn't bear the thought of a Louis loss on June 22, 1938, when, at Yankee Stadium, before a crowd of more than seventy thousand, he and Schmeling squared off for a rematch.

The Brown Bomber pounded Schmeling straight off from the sounding of the round-one bell—pounded, pounded, pounded—for two minutes, four seconds. And the winner is . . .

The man who as a boy couldn't "dream that big" was heavyweight champion of the world for a record twelve straight years, earning millions of dollars. Sadly, he ended up penniless, because he lived too lavishly and made bad business investments. Still, Joe Louis is remembered and idolized for the victor he once was.

■ ■ ■

GWENDOLYN BROOKS

You're going to be the lady Paul Laurence Dunbar!"

Gwendolyn Brooks was seven years old when her mother, Keziah Corinne Wims Brooks, made this proclamation after reading some of her daughter's poems. At the time, Paul Laurence Dunbar (1872–1906) was among the most widely read poets. He was both a starting point and a point of departure for many writers, including Countee Cullen, Jessie Fauset, and Langston Hughes. They were members of the New Negro movement of the 1920s, with its rush of African-centered artistic and political activity (of which the Harlem Renaissance was a part). When young Gwendolyn's mother praised her poems, the New Negro Movement was in full swing.

Mrs. Brooks, a gifted pianist and singer and a former schoolteacher, was not her daughter's only fan. Gwendolyn's love of poetry was also championed by her father, David Anderson Brooks, who supported his family as a janitor at McKinley Music Company. Mr. Brooks delighted Gwendolyn and her little brother, Raymond, with his "story poems," poetry recitations, and storytelling ability. Like his wife, he praised his daughter "to anyone who visited the house."

The Brooks house was on Champlain Avenue in a mostly black section of Chicago, Illinois, known as Bronzeville. In her home, young Gwendolyn spent endless hours reading and writing about what was on her mind and

- **BORN:** *June 17, 1917, in Topeka, Kansas*
- **DIED:** *December 3, 2000, in Chicago, Illinois*

in her heart. Soon, her family, friends, and teachers were not the only people reading her verse. When she was eleven, a local newspaper, the *Hyde Parker*, published several of her poems. When she was thirteen, the children's magazine *American Childhood* published her poem "Eventide." By the time she was sixteen, her poems were appearing weekly in the "Lights and Shadows" column of the *Chicago Defender*, whose chief, Robert Sengstacke Abbott, had helped Bessie Coleman achieve her sky-high dreams.

Encouraging young Gwendolyn's poetic power was one of her idols, Langston Hughes, who gave a poetry recital at the church the Brooks family attended. Mrs. Brooks nudged Gwendolyn to show Hughes some of her poems. Hughes not only took the time to read them but also remarked, "You're very talented! Keep writing! Someday you'll have a book published!"

"Poetry is life distilled."
—Gwendolyn Brooks

Gwendolyn kept reading and writing, kept getting poems published in magazines and anthologies, and kept studying the art of writing in college and in a writing workshop. In time, Hughes's prediction came true: in 1945 Gwendolyn Brooks saw her first collection of poetry, *A Street in Bronzeville*, published. Major recognition came in 1950 when Brooks's second volume of poetry, *Annie Allen*, won the Pulitzer Prize for poetry. She was the first black person to win a Pulitzer.

Poet laureate of Illinois, induction into the NationalWomen's Hall of Fame, recipient of the National Medal of Arts: these are among the many honors and awards Brooks received after 1950 as she produced a novel, her memoirs, and more volumes of poetry (including some for children, among them *Bronzeville Boys and Girls* and *Aloneness*).

Poetry was forever Brooks's first and last passion. Much of her work was about workaday people, such as domestic workers, small-church preachers, laborers, and janitors. Brooks's poems spoke to their sorrows, fears, humiliations, strivings, dreams deferred, and quiet triumphs. Through verse, she protested racism, sexism, classism, and the neglect and abuse of children. She also used her way with words to rally her people to embrace and celebrate their African heritage. She crafted praise-songs to her heroes, too. Among the people Brooks saluted with poems were her father; Paul Robeson; Langston Hughes; Martin Luther King, Jr.; Malcolm X; Chicago's first black mayor, Harold Washington; and the South African poet-activist Keorapetse "Willie" Kgositsile.

Some of Brooks's poems are easy to read; others strain the brain. Her versatility extended to style as well—from Shakespearean sonnets to free verse; from Standard American English to Black English. Her poems sing the blues, echo jazz, and some rock like a folksy sermon.

Brooks spread the word about the power and necessity of poetry in lectures and readings around the world, as well as in workshops and creative writing courses at schools, community centers, prisons, and colleges in America. In the 1960s, she started a workshop for the Blackstone Rangers, a Chicago street gang. Brooks mentored Nikki Giovanni, Carolyn Rodgers, Haki R. Madhubuti (then Don L. Lee), and other talented writers who became major lights of the Black Arts movement, the artistic wing of the black power movement. Over the years Brooks also funded numerous literary awards for people of all ages.

"Her work was sharing and making words matter," said poet and publisher Haki R. Madhubuti at Brooks's funeral. He also said, "She thought we all had possibilities. . . . She wore her love in her language."

■   ■   ■

Jacob Lawrence

When he was thirteen, Harlem was home for Jacob Armstead Lawrence, whom everyone called Jake. And it was in Harlem, with its rich mix of black cultures (southern- and northern-born African-American, West Indian, and African), that Jake discovered his gift for art and came to cherish his heritage.

While Jake was a student at P.S. 68 and at Frederick Douglass Junior High, his mother, a domestic worker, kept her son out of after-school trouble by enrolling him in the Utopia Children's House. There Jake explored a range of creating: soap-making, woodworking, making papier-mâché masks, and painting. His instructor, painter Charles Alston, saw that the teen had talent.

For Jake, art was refuge and respite, escape and exploration, during those days of the Great Depression. When Mrs. Lawrence lost her job, she had to go on public assistance to keep food on the table for Jake and his younger sister and brother. At age sixteen, Jake quit high school and took whatever work he could find (which included delivering laundry). Tough, tight times did not, however, take Jake away from his art.

When Charles Alston opened the Harlem Art Workshop, Jake became a student. He also took classes at the Uptown Art Laboratory (later the Harlem Community Art Center), founded by sculptor and activist Augusta Savage. To deepen his knowledge of art, Jake made frequent visits to

- **BORN:** *September 7, 1917, in Atlantic City, New Jersey*
- **DIED:** *June 9, 2000, in Seattle, Washington*

museums around town. Of all the art he saw at these museums, it was African art that most enthralled.

Jake further educated himself by taking in lectures on black history and culture at the New York Public Library's 135th Street branch. (The original building became part of the Schomburg Center for Research in Black Culture.) He also spent hours reading about black history. And it was to portraying the black experience that Jacob Lawrence devoted most of his talent.

He started with Harlem, capturing the rhythms and ways of her people, from a street preacher to boys making mischief on Halloween. Soon, more people were applauding Lawrence's talent: his brilliant use of primary colors and geometric shapes; his totally original way of creating work so emotionally charged that it not only catches the eye but touches the soul, makes you think, feel, empathize, and sympathize.

"If I have achieved a degree of success as a creative artist, it is mainly due to the black experience, which is our heritage—an experience that gives inspiration, motivation, and stimulation. We do not forget...that encouragement which came from the black community."
—Jacob Lawrence, 1970, upon receiving the NAACP's highest award, the Spingarn Medal

By the time Lawrence was twenty, his work had been exhibited in several group shows and he had won a two-year scholarship to New York City's American Artists School. In 1938, he had a one-man show at the Harlem YMCA. That same year, with Augusta Savage's help, Lawrence secured a job with the Federal Arts Project, one of many government work programs devised during the Great Depression. Lawrence's job was to create two paintings every two weeks for a little under twenty-four dollars per painting.

By then, Lawrence was especially passionate about telling a story in a series of paintings. First came *The Life of Toussaint L'Ouverture* in forty-one paintings, inspired by a production of W. E. B. Du Bois's play *Haiti* that Lawrence had seen. Lawrence also created *The Life of Frederick Douglass*

(thirty-two paintings), *The Life of Harriet Tubman* (thirty-one paintings), and his best-known work, *The Migration of the Negro* (sixty paintings).

Migration recounts the hopes and hazards of the Great Migration (1910–1930), when millions of blacks in the South moved to Chicago, Detroit, East St. Louis, New York City, and other big cities in the West and North in search of better-paying jobs, higher-quality schools, and relief from raw racism. When *Migration* was first exhibited, in December 1941, at the Downtown Gallery in Manhattan, Lawrence became the first black artist in America to have a show at a prestigious white-owned gallery. More of the nation and the world soon discovered what Harlem had known for years: the genius of Jacob Lawrence.

After *Migration*, Lawrence created hundreds more paintings on a range of subjects, including the civil rights movement. With tempera, watercolor, or gouache on paper, hardboard, or illustration board, he also told the equally important "small" stories: those of the labors of everyday people. *The Seamstress* and *The Builders* are among many such paintings. His *Harlem Street Scene* and *The Schomburg Library*, among others, show that Harlem remained dear to his heart.

■   ■   ■

DIZZY GILLESPIE

ebop! Rebop! Or just plain *bop!* These are the names of a snazzier, jazzier jazz that hit the scene in the 1940s, with Dizzy Gillespie among its pioneering players.

This master trumpeter was born John Birks Gillespie. He was the youngest of his parents' nine children, all of whom were early on exposed to music because their father (a bricklayer by day) was the piano man for his weekend band.

John was tinkering on the piano when he was two and a half, but he didn't receive much musical training from his father, who died when John was ten. At age eleven, John started minor music lessons, after an assortment of used instruments arrived at his school. He ended up with a trombone, which he played in a little band put together by his teacher, Miss Wilson.

John was cool with the trombone, until the day he spied, beneath a friend's Christmas tree, a shiny silver-plate trumpet. "I saw that horn and went crazy."

He started spending a lot of time playing his friend's trumpet and pestering Miss Wilson to switch him from trombone to trumpet. Soon, John was playing trumpet in the school band, as well as at local house parties and high school dances with his own band.

The chance for John to dig deeper into music came with a music

- **BORN:** *October 21, 1917, in Cheraw, South Carolina*
- **DIED:** *January 6, 1993, in Englewood, New Jersey*

scholarship to a high school in North Carolina, Laurinburg Institute, where he studied mostly classical music. He kept tight with other sounds by checking out jazz groups that toured in his neck of the woods and by staying steady by the radio for big-band broadcasts. Tops was the Duke Ellington Orchestra, live from Harlem's swanky Cotton Club, where black people could work but couldn't be clientele.

When John's family moved to Philadelphia, Pennsylvania, in 1935, John left school and moved to Philly, too. There he landed a spot in the famous Frankie Fairfax band. It was during his Philly days that, because of his zany, clowning ways onstage—and off—he picked up the nickname "Dizzy."

After a two-year stint with Fairfax, Dizzy Gillespie kicked it to New York, where he hooked up with Teddy Hill's big band. At the time, most jazz musicians had moved away from the original jazz: the "New Orleans sound." Born around 1890, this music was a gumbo of the blues, ragtime, and marching-band music, with an emphasis on group improvisation—and lots of brass, especially trombones and the tuba. By 1930, swing jazz (more mellow, less brassy, so easy to dance to) was the rage, with big bands serving up more regimented—but still hep—music with little room for group improvisation.

> **"I don't care too much about music. What I like is sounds."**
> **—Dizzy Gillespie**

Because swing was so popular, it was the main music of the super-successful band headed up by Thurgood Marshall's high school running buddy, Cab Calloway. Gillespie joined Calloway's New York-based band in 1939.

Calloway cringed whenever Gillespie swung away from swing in his solos. Gillespie kept trying to slip in a new kind of sound; Calloway kept slapping it down. Gillespie got a better hearing for his madcap jazz at after-midnight jam sessions at Minton's Playhouse and other Harlem hot spots.

Jazz had always been up-tempo music, but what Gillespie was pioneering was crazy-fast, with tricky chord shifts, harmonies on the harsh side, a fierce use of an off-pitch blues note—the "flat fifth"—and lots of room for free-styling. Frantic, frenzied, edgy, and at times dizzying, *bebop! rebop! bop!* wasn't music you could dance to.

Many older musicians despised *bebop! rebop! bop!* But Gillespie, alto saxman Charlie "Yardbird" Parker, bebop's "cofounder," and others kept making their maverick music. In a beat, the music wasn't just a hit at jam sessions.

From the mid-1940s to the mid-1950s, bebop was hot—at nightclubs and on concert stages. Dizzy Gillespie was hot, too, gigging with such jazz greats as Ella Fitzgerald and Duke Ellington—and fronting his own bands.

Gillespie was a standout for his stamina, for his ability to pump trumpet pistons faster than folks thought possible, for his crazy pivots and leaps, for pumping Afro-Cuban sounds into the mix, and for classic tunes such as "A Night in Tunisia." Gillespie stood out as well for the look he sported for years: goatee, horn-rimmed specs (or shades), beret at a jaunty angle, and a pin-striped suit. It was a look many mimicked. It was a look of cool.

Cool jazz. Hard bop. Free jazz. Modal jazz. Jazz rock. Post-bop. Neo-bop. The family of jazz had greatly expanded by the late twentieth century. Through it all, Dizzy Gillespie kept groovin' high, performing until he was well into his seventies. He was applauded the world over as an undisputed giant of jazz when he split the scene.

■   ■   ■

SHIRLEY CHISHOLM

The fighting spirit and the nerve to speak up and out were evident early on in the woman born Shirley Anita St. Hill, the oldest of four daughters of a mother from Barbados and a father from Guyana. When very young, Shirley was a pushy, bossy kid. "By the time I was two and half, no bigger than a mite," she wrote, "I was already dominating other children around me—with my mouth. I lectured them and ordered them around. Even Mother was almost afraid of me."

What a terror she might have grown up to be. But she channeled her intensity into positive things. In the supercharged 1960s and 1970s, she was there when the civil rights, black power, women's liberation, and other movements had America in the throes of great change.

With her smarts and her swift way with words, Shirley Chisholm spoke out for equal opportunity for people of color, for women, and for other ignored and slighted Americans. Crowds of people listened to the petite, feisty lady, and many joined her campaign when, on January 25, 1972, she declared herself a candidate for the Democratic Party's nomination for the presidency. Never before in America had a black woman sought to be a major party's presidential candidate.

Chisholm ran a valiant campaign, but she did not receive the party's nomination (George McGovern did). Her run, however, was not a failure, because "Ms. Chis," as she was affectionately called, had rallied more

- **BORN:** *November 30, 1924, in Brooklyn, New York*
- **DIED:** *January 1, 2005, in Ormond Beach, Florida*

women, blacks, Hispanics, and other people of color to get further involved in politics so they could get their concerns heard and have a say about laws that affected their lives.

Chisholm had been making history, making news, and making waves for years. When she sought the Democratic Party's nomination, Chisholm was a member of the House of Representatives (for Brooklyn's Twelfth District), in 1968 having become the first black woman elected to the United States Congress. "Fighting Shirley Chisholm—Unbought and Unbossed" was her campaign slogan.

> "When I was about six or seven... even then I was beginning to show signs of leadership. Only it wasn't called leadership. At that time it was called a rebellious little girl."
> — Shirley Chisholm

From 1968 to 1982, Congresswoman Chisholm crusaded for the needy and the neglected by pushing for, among other things, an increase in the minimum wage, more federal funds for day care centers, decent affordable housing for low-income people, and job training programs for the disabled. One of her proudest moments was passage of a bill she cosponsored for what would be the first monument to a black person in the nation's capital: the statue of Mary McLeod Bethune in Lincoln Park (unveiled July 19, 1974).

Before "Ms. Chis" was Congresswoman Chisholm, she was New York State Assemblywoman Chisholm, the second black woman ever elected to that state's legislature. Extended unemployment insurance for domestic workers and increased funding for public schools were among the causes she championed. Her most prized bill was the one that gave birth to Search for Education, Elevation and Knowledge—better known as SEEK—a program providing poor young people with financial and other types of aid for getting into and staying in college.

Chisholm's concern for young people went way back. Her first career goal was to be a teacher. That's what she became, at a nursery school in Harlem, after she graduated—with honors—from Brooklyn College. While she taught, she continued learning at Columbia University (at night), earning a master's degree in elementary education in 1952. In 1953, she became director of the Hamilton-Madison Child Care Center in lower Manhattan. After six years on that job she went to work for the New York City Bureau of Child Welfare, as a consultant on day care.

Politics had been in Chisholm's blood since her college days, when she attended political rallies and meetings and did volunteer work for several civil rights organizations, including the National Urban League and the National Association for the Advancement of Colored People. She later became involved with several Democratic Party organizations, learning more about how politics was played. This prepared her to run for the assembly, which gave her the know-how and the courage to run for Congress, which in turn emboldened her to one day make a bid for her nation's highest office.

■ ■ ■

MALCOLM X

He was in his mother's womb on the early spring night in 1925 when hooded Ku Klux Klansmen galloped around his family's home in Omaha, Nebraska, shooting off their guns and smashing windows. It was a get-out-of-town message for Malcolm's father, Earl Little, who happened to be out of town when the KKK terrified his pregnant wife, Louise, and their three children.

Mr. Little was the Midwest organizer for the Universal Negro Improvement Association, founded by Marcus Garvey, of Jamaica. Garvey promoted black unity, black pride, and a love for Africa—ideas many whites found threatening.

Malcolm was three years old on the frightfully cold November night that black-robed terrorists torched the Little home in Lansing, Michigan. The Littles lost everything but their lives. They moved again, to the outskirts of East Lansing.

Malcolm was six (with six siblings by then) when on a late September night his mother's screams woke him up: Mrs. Little had just been told that her husband had been run over by a trolley car. His skull was crushed, his body torn almost in two. The authorities labeled it an accident, but Malcolm would forever believe his father had been murdered by the type of people who had terrorized his family before.

Malcolm did what he could to help his family survive: fishing, hunting

- **BORN:** *May 19, 1925, in Omaha, Nebraska*
- **DIED:** *February 21, 1965, in New York City*

rabbits, and sometimes pinching food from a grocery store. He even tried to find some victory in boxing, after Joe Louis became heavyweight champion in 1937—"Every Negro boy old enough to walk wanted to be the next Brown Bomber," he later recalled.

Malcolm's troubles increased when his mother was committed to a mental institution and the Little children were put into foster care. When Malcolm began acting up in school, he ended up in a juvenile home.

Malcolm didn't want to be bad. He kept trying to be good; he had dreams of making something of himself—a lawyer perhaps. That's what he told his eighth-grade English (and favorite) teacher, Mr. Ostrowski.

"We all here like you," responded Mr. Ostrowski. "But you've got to be realistic about being a nigger. A lawyer—that's no realistic goal for a nigger."

Malcolm was through—with Mr. Ostrowski, with school, with trying to be good, and soon with Michigan, too.

A slickster, a hipster, that's what Malcolm became. Pool halls, bars, and nightclubs were his chief hangouts; numbers running, pimping, dope dealing, and boosting, his way of life—in Boston, New York City, and elsewhere—until, at twenty-two, he landed in prison for armed robbery.

When he was released at age twenty-seven, Malcolm Little had educated himself by taking correspondence courses, by copying the pages of a dictionary, and by reading books from the prison library: philosophy, history, sociology, anthropology, autobiography. He had also become a follower of the Nation of Islam (NOI), which advocated clean living and many of the principles Marcus Garvey had preached, along with the idea that white people were "devils." As a member of NOI, Malcolm discarded his surname and replaced it with an "X," which, for NOI members,

> "Education is an important element in the struggle for Human Rights. It is the means to help our children and our people rediscover their identity and thereby increase their self-respect. Education is our passport to the future, for tomorrow belongs to the people who prepare for it today."
> —*Malcolm X*

"symbolized the true African family name that [they] never could know." By the mid-1950s, the extremely articulate, very charismatic Malcolm X was NOI's national spokesperson and based in New York City.

In magazine interviews, on radio and television shows, and at street-corner rallies, Malcolm X stridently condemned white America for failing to repent for nearly 250 years of slavery followed by 100 years of Jim Crow—for all the years of stolen labor, brutal treatment, indifference to white-on-black violence, and everything else bound up in the filthy word *nigger*. He urged his people to learn their history and to embrace the African in them. Integration was not the way, Malcolm proclaimed.

Malcolm X was thirty-seven years old when he began to question the righteousness of NOI and its leader, Elijah Muhammad. After Malcolm X left NOI, he founded the Organization of Afro-American Unity (OAAU). He also did quite a bit of traveling abroad, learning more about the world and lecturing on human rights. In Ghana, one of his treasured experiences was a luncheon with W. E. B. Du Bois's widow, writer and activist Shirley Graham Du Bois. After Malcolm X's pilgrimage *(hajj)* to the Muslim holy site of Mecca in Saudi Arabia, he ceased believing that all white people were "devils."

He returned to America a Sunni Muslim and with a new name: El-Hajj Malik El-Shabazz. This forty-year-old man was poised to become a more powerful agent of social change when three men gunned him down as he delivered a speech at an OAAU rally at Harlem's Audubon Ballroom.

In the front row sat his four young daughters and his wife, Betty, with twin girls in her womb.

■ ■ ■

MARTIN LUTHER KING, JR

He was thrown into jail several times. He was stabbed in the chest in New York City. He dodged rocks and bottles in Chicago, Illinois. In various cities in the South—*again and again and again*—he faced water cannons and police dogs whose masters relished opportunities to bang billy clubs upside black heads.

He had to contend with repeated reports of civil rights workers being beaten, being murdered; with his home being bombed; with the Ku Klux Klan burning crosses on his lawn; with the FBI tapping his phone; with constant death threats.

All this because he preached.

He preached that racism—individual and government-sponsored—was ungodly. He preached that it was a sin for a nation as wealthy as America to allow millions of her citizens to languish in poverty—low-grade schools, shoddy housing, children going to bed hungry. He preached against America's involvement in the war between North and South Vietnam. He preached love and peace, and the "beloved community."

Martin Luther King, Jr., did not start the civil rights movement, but he definitely was the person who emerged in the mid-twentieth century as the movement's most commanding spokesperson. He summoned thousands to the campaign: children, teens, adults; Christians, Jews, and those of other faiths; and people of every hue. With his glorious oratory and his

- **BORN:** *January 15, 1929, in Atlanta, Georgia*
- **DIED:** *April 4, 1968, in Memphis, Tennessee*

knowledge of the holy, King roused people to risk harm and death in demonstrations, sit-ins, and other forms of nonviolent protest. His efforts to redeem the soul of America were applauded by enlightened people around the world, and most prominently praised in 1964, when he was awarded the Nobel Peace Prize.

Fame was not something King had coveted when he was a boy growing up in a middle-class section of Atlanta, Georgia. He was the son, grandson, and great-grandson of Baptist ministers, so chances were that he would enter the ministry, too, and live a fairly comfortable life pastoring a middle-class church. No one envisioned a wider calling.

> "True peace is not merely the absence of tension; it is the presence of justice."
> —*Martin Luther King, Jr.*

King himself did not have an inkling while he was excelling in primary and secondary school (doing well enough to be admitted to college at age fifteen), nor while he was earning degrees at Morehouse College, in Atlanta, Georgia (bachelor's degree in sociology); Crozer Seminary in Chester, Pennsylvania (bachelor of divinity); and Boston University (doctorate in systematic theology).

Neither was King looking to be in the limelight when, on December 1, 1955, news spread that a hardworking forty-three-year-old seamstress had declared, in essence, *No, I won't give up my seat so a white man can sit down!*—and had been tossed in jail. Out of Rosa Parks's defiance of a racist statute arose a boycott of public buses in Montgomery, Alabama, where twenty-six-year-old Martin Luther King, Jr., was pastor of Dexter Avenue Baptist Church. King did not jockey for a leadership position in this boycott, but he was the one chosen.

Death threats came fast and frequently. In late January 1956 an anonymous telephone caller threatened, "Nigger, we are tired of you and your mess now. And if you aren't out of this town in three days, we're going to blow your brains out and blow up your house."

King was shaken, and so he prayed; alone, around midnight, in his

kitchen, he prayed. "Lord, I'm down here trying to do what's right.... But Lord, I must confess that I'm weak now. I'm faltering. I'm losing my courage." He prayed a little longer and then, he said, "It seemed...that I could hear an inner voice saying to me, 'Martin Luther, stand up for righteousness. Stand up for justice. Stand up for truth. And lo I will be with you, even until the end of the world'....I heard the voice of Jesus saying still to fight on."

Fight on he did, even when, three days after that nasty phone call, his home was bombed. Fight on he did, in a bus boycott that lasted 382 days, sparked bus boycotts in other southern cities, and led to the United States Supreme Court outlawing segregation on public transportation.

Fight on he did, long after the boycott, for more than a decade—in sit-ins, in marches, in jail, in radio and television interviews, in speeches, in meetings with President John Kennedy and other VIPs, and at the epic March on Washington in 1963. Fight on he did, speaking truth to power and to the powerless as well—until the moment an assassin's bullet brought him down. Because he preached.

■ ■ ■

Charlayne Hunter-Gault

On June 11, 1988, tall, queenly Charlayne Hunter-Gault, with her beautiful southern drawl, delivered the commencement address at the University of Georgia (UGA), in Athens. And what a historic moment that was.

Since its founding in 1785, the university had never had a black person give the graduation address. How fitting it was that Charlayne Hunter-Gault was the first. In 1961, after a nearly two-year legal campaign waged by the NAACP Legal Defense and Educational Fund, she and Hamilton Holmes (a future doctor) became UGA's first black students.

"Two, four six, eight, / We don't want to integrate." That's what a group of students chanted outside Charlayne's rooms on the UGA campus one September night in 1961. On another night, a brick and a soda bottle came crashing through her window.

"Those were times of testing," Hunter-Gault told UGA's class of 1988, "and, yes, of triumph. Of pioneering and legend-building. Of armor-building."

The hostility and the publicity that surrounded this young newsmaker steeled her resolve to become a journalist. It was a dream sparked by a childhood fascination with the comic-strip ace reporter Brenda Starr. Charlayne was even more keen on journalism after working on the newspaper at Henry McNeal Turner High School, in Atlanta, Georgia, where she spent most of her youth.

Her childhood was filled with people who praised her potential, and

■ **Born**: *February 27, 1942, in Due West, South Carolina*

helped her develop the backbone to aim high and stay proud in the face of enormous propaganda about black inferiority. Chief among her boosters and role models was her maternal grandmother, an intelligent, curious, though unschooled woman who read three newspapers a day.

"My ideal woman—smart and strong, creative and feminine" is how Charlayne Hunter-Gault described her mother. Charlayne's father, an army chaplain, constantly applauded Charlayne's "first-rate mind" and constantly charged her not to let it dull. He also instilled in her the idea that she was not to be denied.

He made this point most forcefully when the family was, for a short while, living in Alaska, where he was stationed. One day, Charlayne and some white schoolmates went to a club for the children of army officers. Charlayne was refused admission based on the assumption that she was the daughter of an enlisted man. Instead of making it clear that her father was an officer and she therefore had every right to be in the club, twelve-year-old Charlayne shrank away.

> "No one ever told me not to dream, and when the time came to act on that dream, I would not let anything stand in the way of fulfilling it."
> —*Charlayne Hunter-Gault*

"You have to let these people know who you are," her father declared after he found out about the incident. "You can't let them deny you. . . . Go if you want. Don't go if you don't want to. But the choice is yours, not theirs."

By the time Charlayne graduated from UGA, with a bachelor's degree in journalism, she was determined not to be denied a career in her chosen field. And by the time she delivered that commencement address at UGA, Charlayne Hunter-Gault had distinguished herself as a print and broadcast journalist.

Her journey had included writing for *The New Yorker* magazine and a ten-year stint as a reporter for *The New York Times*, serving as the newspaper's Harlem bureau chief for two of those years. In 1978 Hunter-Gault became a correspondent for the half-hour PBS news program *The MacNeil/Lehrer Report*. Five years later, she was named national correspondent for the program, which had expanded to *The MacNeil/Lehrer NewsHour*. Her numerous awards and honors include being named Journalist of the Year by the National Association of Black Journalists in 1986. That same year she received the coveted George Foster Peabody Award for Excellence in Broadcast Journalism for her *NewsHour*

series, "Apartheid's People," about the years of justice denied to people of color in South Africa.

Near the close of her speech at UGA on that spring day in 1988, Hunter-Gault urged the graduates not to shrink from their potential to make America a more "perfect union," a nation where no woman, no man, no child is denied opportunities solely because of race, ethnicity, gender, or for any other reason. And she ended with some lines from Gwendolyn Brooks's poem "Paul Robeson": "We are each other's harvest, / We are each other's business, / We are each other's magnitude / And bond."

In 1997, Charlayne Hunter-Gault moved to South Africa, where she carried on with her career as a journalist, working as a correspondent for National Public Radio and then as CNN's Johannesburg bureau chief.

■   ■   ■

JUDITH JAMISON

When I was six years old, I was tall, lean, and long-legged," Judith Jamison wrote in her autobiography, *Dancing Spirit.* "At ten I could walk down the street and see over everybody's head. I loved being last on line in elementary school and peeking at what was happening up front."

Had young Judith been uptight about her height, she might have missed her calling. She might have hunched, slumped, and made herself shy. Thankfully, she did not suffer from low self-esteem. The only thing young Judith "suffered from" was boundless energy.

It was her hyperactivity that, in part, prompted her parents to enroll six-year-old Judith in Philadelphia's Judimar School of Dance. There she studied classical ballet, jazz, tap, and acrobatics (which she didn't much like). She was also introduced to movements rooted in African dance, something she became more intrigued with when she saw a lecture-demonstration by anthropologist and choreographer Pearl Primus, who specialized in African dance. "[Pearl Primus] brought the black woman's power and knowledge to the stage....She had gone to [Africa], which impressed me as a ten-year-old, and I was blown away by her performance."

After Judith graduated from high school, she spent about a year in limbo before enrolling in Nashville, Tennessee's Fisk University, where she planned to major in psychology. Her dancing spirit had other plans. After

- **BORN:** *May 10, 1943, in Philadelphia, Pennsylvania*

three semesters at Fisk, it whisked her back to Philadelphia and into the Philadelphia Dance Academy (which became part of what is now the University of the Arts).

While attending the academy, Jamison first saw a performance by the startlingly original dance troupe Alvin Ailey had founded in the late 1950s—a company that focused on black themes and specialized in the moves and music of American choreographers and composers.

The Alvin Ailey American Dance Theater was utterly refreshing. Alvin Ailey in motion astounded Judith Jamison: "Nobody danced like Alvin. He moved like quicksilver." Minnie Marshall's performance in Ailey's masterpiece, *Revelations*, also inspired Jamison. "I looked at Minnie onstage and thought to myself, 'I can do that.'"

Jamison had even more of the can-do spirit after a class with Agnes de Mille. This legendary white dancer and choreographer saw something extra-special in Jamison. De Mille invited Jamison to perform in a ballet of hers, which would debut at New York City's Lincoln Center in the spring of 1965.

> "Dance is vulnerability, it's about giving your love, light, generosity. If an audience can pick up on all these things when you're on stage, then you're doing your job."
> —*Judith Jamison*

Jamison was thrilled to move to New York City, thrilled to be cast in de Mille's *The Four Marys*, which featured another of Jamison's idols, Carmen de Lavallade, a frequent guest artist in Alvin Ailey's troupe. Not long after *The Four Marys* closed, Jamison heard that choreographer Donald McKayle (a Pearl Primus protégé) was auditioning dancers for a television special hosted by calypso king Harry Belafonte.

"I was dreadful. . . . I hadn't danced the entire summer and I was in very bad shape." Jamison left the audition in tears, and with a creeping fear that she might have to pack away her ballet slippers. Fortunately, a few days after that awful audition, she received a call from someone who had heard about her potential and wanted her to join his company:

Alvin Ailey. Jamison was never "dreadful" again. In time, she became the principal dancer of Ailey's troupe.

When Jamison began with Ailey's company, black studies courses and departments were emerging on college campuses, and increasing numbers of black people of all ages were learning about their history and connecting to their African heritage. The five-foot-ten Jamison, so strong and regal, with her natural hair and her absolute delight in her rich dark skin, was a stunning symbol of the black consciousness movement.

For some fifteen years, as a member of Ailey's troupe, Jamison took the "black woman's power"—and many Pearl Primus dances—to stages across the nation and around the world, including in Africa. The dance that catapulted Jamison to superstardom was one Alvin Ailey created especially for her: *Cry,* a sixteen-minute solo about the tribulations and triumphs of black women in America.

In 1980, Jamison left Ailey's company to star in a Broadway musical, *Sophisticated Ladies.* During the 1980s, she also guest-starred with other dance companies, channeled her dancing spirit into choreography, and launched her own dance company, the Jamison Project.

When Alvin Ailey fell ill in 1989, Jamison returned to his company to serve as associate director. In late December 1989, a few weeks after Ailey died, and as he had wished, Jamison became the company's artistic director, devoting her incredible energy to keeping the company alive and vital.

■　■　■

RUTH SIMMONS

When, in 2001, *60 Minutes* correspondent Morley Safer asked Ruth Simmons about the value of education, she made it clear that she did not regard education as merely a means of acquiring a good or better job and making heaps of money. "Education is here to nourish your soul," she stressed. "Education transforms your life." Of this, her soul is definitely a witness.

She was born Ruth Jean Stubblefield in a rural East Texas town, where her parents made a meager living as sharecroppers. Her family stayed poor when they moved to Houston, where her father was a factory worker and her mother a maid.

"I never had a toy when I was growing up. . . . For Christmas we would get a shoe box with about ten nuts, an orange, and an apple."

"We" was herself and eleven siblings. But the Stubblefield children would not be pulverized by poverty, nor by the racism that was so intense when they were growing up. This was because their parents instilled in them principles that would forge character and make them strong. For Ruth, the baby of the family, school was also a huge rescue.

When Ruth entered kindergarten, she met her first mentor: her teacher, Ida Mae Henderson. This woman discerned right away how bright Ruth was. Henderson gave the angel-faced girl everlasting encouragement, which helped her contend with being called "bookworm" and with schoolmates making fun of her clothes.

▪ **BORN:** *July 3, 1945, in Diley, Texas*

Grade after grade, other teachers rooted for Ruth. When she was bound for Dillard University in New Orleans, Louisiana, in the fall of 1963, several teachers at Phillis Wheatley High sent her off with more than well wishes: along with money, they gave her clothes out of their own closets.

The "bookworm" went on to do them—and her family—proud: she graduated from Dillard, summa cum laude, with a bachelor's degree in French literature; she earned, from Harvard University, a doctorate in Romance languages and literatures (by which time she was a few years into her marriage to lawyer and entrepreneur Norbert Simmons).

From the early 1970s on, Ruth Simmons distinguished herself as a professor and as an administrator at several institutions of higher learning, including Princeton University and Spelman College. Simmons inspired students to excellence and to lifelong learning. She gave wise counsel to the homesick, the unsure, and the over-confident. She rallied faculty members to give teaching their all. She championed diversity and promoted racial harmony

"Nothing is so beautiful, nothing so moving, as the observance of a mind at work." —Ruth Simmons

on campuses where racial strife existed. She staunchly defended the value of a liberal arts education, while so many others deemed it not "practical," arguing that studies that lead to top-paying jobs should be a student's first focus. Intelligent, compassionate, principled, and disciplined—these are just some of the words students and colleagues used in their praise and appreciation of Simmons.

In 1995, Ruth Simmons made history when she became the first black person appointed to the presidency of Smith College, the elite women's college in Northampton, Massachusetts. With all the "Congratulations!" from VIPs that Simmons received, there were also precious letters from youngsters whose lives were similar to that of little Ruth Jean Stubblefield. One girl wrote that although her parents had told her she could achieve great things, she had not really believed it until she saw a newspaper article about Simmons.

Simmons became front-page news again in late 2000, when she was appointed the first black president of an Ivy League school: Brown University in Providence, Rhode Island. Simmons, the great-granddaughter of enslaved people, became not only the first black but also the first female president of this university. The appointment was doubly significant: the school, originally Rhode Island College—and for men only—when founded in the 1760s, had changed its name to Brown in the early 1800s, after receiving a hefty donation from the Providence merchant Nicholas Brown, whose wealth derived in part from his business as a slave trader.

"I would not have thought it possible for a person of my background to become the president of Brown University," said Simmons when she was named Brown's eighteenth president. But the seemingly impossible had happened, serving as a mighty reminder to boys and girls enduring disadvantages that they, too, could achieve awesome things.

■　■　■

BEN CARSON

D ummy." That's what some of his fifth-grade classmates called
the skinny little boy whose mother called him Bennie.

"You weren't born to be a failure, Bennie," Mrs. Carson
stressed to her ten-year-old son. He had begun to dream of being
a doctor, but in fifth grade, even getting a D in math was a struggle. "You
can't settle for just barely passing. You're too smart to do that."

His mother helped him along by quizzing him on the multiplication
tables at the end of her long workday. At times, she worked two and three
jobs to shelter, feed, and clothe him and his older brother, Curtis. When
Bennie and Curtis's parents divorced, Mr. Carson wasn't faithful when it
came to child support.

Mrs. Carson encouraged both her sons to *read, read, read*. She even
went so far as to require them to read at least two books a week, with
book reports part of the assignment. "If you can read, honey, you can
learn just about anything you want to know," said Mrs. Carson, who had
only a third-grade education. "The doors of the world are open to people
who can read."

Bennie became a spectacular reader. His vocabulary grew large. He
improved in math, too. He was excellent in his favorite subject: science.
Then, in junior high school, Bennie began to slip.

He got fed up with other kids "capping" on him because of his low-budget

■ **BORN:** *September 18, 1951, in Detroit, Michigan*

clothes, so he started to cap back, developing a razor-sharp tongue. Bennie badgered his mother constantly for clothes considered cool in Detroit and elsewhere in the mid-1960s. "Italian knit shirts with suede fronts" were high on Bennie's list, as were "silk pants, thick-and-thin silk socks, alligator shoes, stingy-brim hats, leather jackets, and suede coats."

Instead of going straight home after school, Bennie was hitting the streets, staying out sometimes until eleven o'clock at night. Not surprisingly, he ended up a C student. Worse, he developed a terrible temper. When he and another student got into a little dispute at their lockers one day, Bennie bashed the boy in the forehead with his combination lock.

"I'm not going to wear these ugly things," Bennie yelled at his mother after throwing at her an uncool pair of pants she had just bought him. When Mrs. Carson tried to reason with him, he sassed her some more. He was on the verge of hitting his mother when his brother jumped in and held him back.

> "Listen and learn from people who have already been where you want to go. Benefit from their mistakes instead of repeating them."
> —Ben Carson

His temper, it seemed, couldn't be tamed. "Totally without thinking, when my anger was aroused," he later wrote, "I grabbed the nearest brick, rock, or stick to bash someone."

When Bennie and a friend got into a tiff over which radio station they would listen to, he responded by "grabbing the camping knife I carried in my back pocket.... With all the power of my young muscles, I thrust the knife toward his belly."

Thankfully, there was a big, thick belt buckle between the knife and his friend's belly. Realizing that he could have seriously injured—and possibly killed—his friend, Bennie was ready to make a change.

At home, Bennie returned to something his mother had taught him to do when he was very young: "Pray. My mother had taught me to pray." After he prayed, he turned to the Holy Bible and began reading the book of Proverbs. He lingered at Proverbs 16:32: "He who is slow to anger is better than the mighty; and he who rules his spirit than he who takes a city." Fourteen-year-old Benjamin Solomon Carson was back on track.

Carson's scholastic achievements in high school earned him a scholarship to Yale University. After Yale, he attended the University of Michigan Medical School, where he became extremely interested in surgery on the nervous system. Recognizing his fascination with the human brain and his terrific hand-eye coordination, he decided to become a neurosurgeon. Hands once so quick to harm would be devoted to healing people—specifically, children.

In 1984, the thirty-three-year-old Dr. Carson became director of pediatric surgery at the prestigious Johns Hopkins Hospital in Baltimore, Maryland. Three years later, he became internationally known as the lead surgeon in the first successful separation of Siamese twins joined at the back of the head. The twins were seven months old. Carson and his colleagues had spent five months planning that surgery, which lasted twenty-two hours.

Ben Carson went on to help and heal many other children. He also inspired people through his books, which include his autobiography, *Gifted Hands,* and *Think Big: Unleashing Your Potential for Excellence.* Establishing the Carson Scholars Fund in 1994 was just one way the good doctor committed himself to helping young achievers make the most of their brain power.

■   ■   ■

Source Notes

◆ Frederick Douglass

"If a slave...abolished." Frederick Douglass, *Narrative of the Life of Frederick Douglass* (1845), in Henry Louis Gates, ed., *Frederick Douglass: Autobiographies* (New York: Library of America, 1994), p. 43.

"From...fellow-slaves." Frederick Douglass, ibid., p. 43.

"rigged...style." Frederick Douglass, *Life and Times of Frederick Douglass* (1893), ibid., p. 644.

"The American...will be safe." Frederick Douglass, "Southern Barbarism" (April 1886) in Frederick S. Voss, *Majestic in His Wrath: A Pictorial Life of Frederick Douglass* (Washington, D.C.: Smithsonian Institution Press, 1995), p. 81.

◆ Matthew Henson

"There can be...worthwhile." Matthew Henson, quoted on http://www.motivateus.com.

"The commander...finished." Matthew Henson, *A Negro Explorer at the North Pole* (1912). Reprint. (New York: Cooper Square Press, 2001), p. 136.

◆ W.E.B. Du Bois

"I believe in...selves." W.E.B. Du Bois, "Credo" (1904) in David Levering Lewis, ed., *W.E.B. Du Bois: A Reader* (New York: Holt, 1995), p. 88.

◆ Mary McLeod Bethune

"My feet...here." Mary McLeod Bethune, quoted in Malu Halasa, *Mary McLeod Bethune: Educator* (New York: Chelsea House, 1989), p. 65.

"We burned...elderberries." Mary McLeod Bethune, quoted in Tonya Bolden, *And Not Afraid to Dare: The Stories of Ten African-American Women* (New York: Scholastic, 1998), p. 101.

"If I...love." Mary McLeod Bethune, "My Last Will and Testament," *Ebony* magazine (August 1955).

◆ Bessie Coleman

"TELL THEM...TO FLY!" Bessie Coleman, quoted in Doris L. Rich, *Queen Bess: Daredevil Aviator* (Washington, D.C.: Smithsonian Institution Press, 1993), p. 70.

"If...no regrets." Bessie Coleman, ibid., p. 114.

◆ Paul Robeson

"No one...to himself." Paul Robeson, quoted in Dorothy Winbush Riley, ed., *My Soul Looks Back, 'Less I Forget: A Collection of Quotations by People of Color* (New York: HarperCollins, 1993), p. 414.

◆ Satchel Paige

"I was...Fame." Satchel Paige, quoted in Michael MacCambridge, ed., *ESPN SportsCentury* (New York: Hyperion ESPN Books, 1999), p. 121.

◆ Thurgood Marshall

"I...shortened it." Thurgood Marshall, quoted in Lisa Aldred, *Thurgood Marshall: Supreme Court Justice* (New York: Chelsea House, 1990), p. 23.

"Before...by heart." Thurgood Marshall, ibid., p. 27.

"That he...had." Thurgood Marshall, quoted in Deirdre Mullane, ed., *Words to Make My Dream Children Live: A Book of African American Quotations* (New York: Anchor, 1995), p. 314.

◆ Pauli Murray

"I speak for...just people." Pauli Murray, *Dark Testament and Other Poems* (1970), quoted in Caroline F. Ware, Epilogue, *Song in a Weary Throat: An American Pilgrimage* (New York: Harper & Row, 1987), p. 437.

"Their striving...incentive." Pauli Murray, ibid., p. 1.

◆ Joe Louis

"I couldn't...big." Joe Louis, quoted in Jim Campbell, *The Importance of Joe Louis* (San Diego: Lucent Books, 1997), p. 15.

"Don't jab...through it." Joe Louis, quoted in Wilfrid Sheed, "Joe Louis and Babe Didrikson," *ESPN SportsCentury* (New York: Hyperion ESPN Books, 1999), p. 106.

◆ Gwendolyn Brooks

"You're...Dunbar!" Keziah Wims Brooks, quoted in Gwendolyn Brooks, *Report from Part Two* (Chicago: Third World Press, 1996), p. 11.

"You're...a book published!" Langston Hughes, ibid., p. 12.

"Poetry...distilled." Gwendolyn Brooks, quoted in Brian Lanker, *I Dream a World: Portraits of Black Women Who Changed America* (New York: Stewart, Tabori & Chang, 1989), p. 43.

"Her work...her language." Haki R. Madhubuti, quoted in *Essence* (March 2001). Reprint. http://www.findarticles.com.

◆ Jacob Lawrence

"If...black community." Jacob Lawrence, quoted in Paul J. Karlstrom, "Jacob Lawrence: Modernism, Race, and Community." In Peter T. Nesbett and Michelle DuBois, eds., *Over the Line: The Art and Life of Jacob Lawrence* (Seattle: University of Washington Press, 2000), p. 229.

◆ Dizzy Gillespie

"I saw...crazy." Dizzy Gillespie, quoted in Alyn Shipton, *Groovin' High: The Life of Dizzy Gillespie* (New York: Oxford University Press, 1999), p. 9.

"I don't...sounds." Dizzy Gillespie in an interview in Stockholm, August 1970, quoted in Mullane, *Words to Make My Dream Children Live*, p. 175.

◆ Shirley Chisholm

"By...afraid of me." Shirley Chisholm, *Unbought and Unbossed* (Boston: Houghton, Mifflin, 1970), pp. 3–4.

"When...little girl." Shirley Chisholm, quoted in Lanker, *I Dream a World*, p. 106.

◆ Malcolm X

"Every...Brown Bomber." Malcolm X, *The Autobiography of Malcolm X*, as told to Alex Haley (New York: Grove Press, 1965), p. 23.

"Education...today." Malcolm X, "Organization of Afro-American Unity: A Statement of Basic Aims and Objectives" (June 1964), reprinted in John Henrik Clarke, ed., *Malcolm X: The Man and His Times* (Trenton, NJ: Africa World Press, 1990), p. 337.

"We all...nigger." Mr. Ostrowski, in *The Autobiography of Malcolm X*, p. 37.

"symbolized...never know." Malcolm X, ibid., p. 201.

◆ Martin Luther King, Jr.

"True peace...justice." Martin Luther King, Jr., *Stride Toward Freedom* (1958), quoted in Riley, *My Soul Looks Back*, p. 302.

"Nigger...your house." Martin Luther King, Jr., quoted in David J. Garrow, *Bearing the Cross: Martin Luther King, Jr., and the Southern Christian Leadership Conference* (New York: Morrow, 1986), pp. 57–58.

"Lord...fight on." Martin Luther King, Jr., ibid., p. 58.

◆ Charlayne Hunter-Gault

"Two...integrate." Quoted in Charlayne Hunter-Gault, *In My Place* (New York: Vintage, 1993), p. 178.

"Those...armor-building." Charlayne Hunter-Gault, ibid., p. 249.

"ideal woman...feminine." Charlayne Hunter-Gault, ibid., in caption following p. 116.

"first-rate mind." Mr. Hunter, ibid., p. 93.

"No...fulfilling it." Charlayne Hunter-Gault, ibid., p. 2.

"You...not theirs." Mr. Hunter, ibid., p. 97.

"We are...bond." Gwendolyn Brooks, "Paul Robeson," *Blacks* (Chicago: Third World Press, 1991), p. 496.

◆ Judith Jamison

"When I was...front." Judith Jamison, *Dancing Spirit: An Autobiography*, with Howard Kaplan (New York: Doubleday, 1993), p. 5.

"[Pearl Primus} brought...her performance." Judith Jamison, ibid., p. 29.

"Nobody danced like...that.'" Judith Jamison, ibid., p. 53.

"Dance...your job." Judith Jamison, quoted in Riley, *My Soul Looks Back*, p. 221.

"I was...shape." Judith Jamison, *Dancing Spirit*, p. 64.

◆ Ruth Simmons

"Education...life." Ruth Simmons, "President Simmons." *60 Minutes* (24 June 2001).

"I never had...apple." Ruth Simmons, ibid.

"Nothing is...work." Ruth Simmons, Inaugural Address, 14 October 2001, quoted on http://www.brown.edu.

One girl wrote...Simmons. "Simmons, Ruth J." *Current Biography Yearbook 1996* (Bronx, NY: H.W. Wilson, 1997) p. 515.

"I would...Brown University." Ruth Simmons, *60 Minutes*.

◆ Ben Carson

"You...Bennie." Sonya Carson, quoted in Ben Carson, M.D., with Cecil Murphey, *Gifted Hands: The Ben Carson Story* (Grand Rapids, MI: Zondervan, 1990), p. 18.

"You can't...do that." Sonya Carson, ibid., p. 33.

"If you...can read." Sonya Carson, ibid., p. 37.

"Italian knit...and suede coats." Ben Carson, ibid., p. 49.

"I'm not...ugly things." Ben Carson, ibid., p. 55.

"Listen and learn...them." Ben Carson, ibid., p. 226.

"Totally...to bash someone." Ben Carson, ibid., p. 56.

"grabbing...toward his belly." Ben Carson, ibid., p. 56.

"Pray...to pray." Ben Carson, ibid., p. 57.

Suggested Reading

(for ages ten and up)

Aldred, Lisa. *Thurgood Marshall: Supreme Court Justice*. New York: Chelsea House, 1990.

Beals, Melba Patillo. *Warriors Don't Cry: A Searing Memoir of the Battle to Integrate Little Rock's Central High*. Abridged. Edited by Anne Greenberg. New York: Pocket, 1995.

Campbell, Jim. *The Importance of Joe Louis*. San Diego: Lucent Books, 1997.

Carson, Ben, M.D., with Cecil Murphey. *Gifted Hands: The Ben Carson Story*. Grand Rapids, MI: Zondervan, 1990.

Clinton, Catherine, ed. *I, Too, Sing America: Three Centuries of African American Poetry*. Boston: Houghton Mifflin, 1998.

Cox, Clinton. *African American Healers*. New York: Wiley, 1999.

———. *African American Teachers*. New York: Wiley, 2000.

Editors of Time-Life Books. *African Americans: Voices of Triumph*. 3 vols. Alexandria, VA: Time-Life, 1994.

Gilman, Michael. *Matthew Henson: Explorer*. New York: Chelsea House, 1988.

Gorrell, Gena K. *North Star to Freedom: The Story of the Underground Railroad*. New York: Delacorte, 1997.

Halasa, Malu. *Mary McLeod Bethune: Educator*. New York: Chelsea House, 1989.

Hansen, Joyce. *Women of Hope: African Americans Who Made a Difference*. New York: Scholastic, 1998.

Hart, Philip S. *Up in the Air: The Story of Bessie Coleman*. Minneapolis: Carolrhoda Books, 1996.

Haskins, Jim. *Black Eagles: African Americans in Aviation*. New York: Scholastic, 1997.

———. *Black Stars of the Harlem Renaissance*. New York: Scholastic, 2002.

Hine, Darlene Clark, and Clayborne Carson, senior consulting eds. *Milestones in Black American History*. New York: Chelsea House, 1994–1996.

Kelley, Robin D. G., and Earl Lewis, general eds. *The Young Oxford History of African Americans*. New York: Oxford University Press, 1995–1997.

King, Casey, and Linda Barrett Osborne; portraits by Joe Brooks; foreword by Rosa Parks. *Oh, Freedom! Kids Talk About the Civil Rights Movement with the People Who Made It Happen*. New York: Knopf, 1997.

McKissack, Patricia C., and Fredrick McKissack, Jr. *Black Diamond: The Story of the Negro Baseball Leagues*. New York: Scholastic, 1994.

Myers, Walter Dean. *The Great Migration: An American Story*. Paintings by Jacob Lawrence, with a poem in appreciation. New York: The Museum of Modern Art, The Phillips Collection, HarperCollins, 1993.

———. *Malcolm X: By Any Means Necessary*. New York: Scholastic, 1993.

Pinkney, Andrea Davis. *Let It Shine: Stories of Black Women Freedom Fighters*. New York: Harcourt, 2000.

Rochelle, Belinda, ed. *Words with Wings: A Treasury of African-American Poetry and Art*. New York: HarperCollins/Amistad, 2001.

Stafford, Mark. *W.E.B. Du Bois: Scholar and Activist*. New York: Chelsea House, 1989.

Sullivan, Charles, ed. *Children of Promise: African-American Literature and Art for Young People*. New York: Harry N. Abrams, 1991.

Wilkinson, Brenda. *African American Women Writers*. New York: Wiley, 2000.